About the Autho

Dr Katharine McGarry is a Developmental Neuropsychologist who gained her Ph.D. from the University of Birmingham in 2014. The author currently holds a Senior University Lecturer position where she regularly publishes on topics relating to developmental psychology, mental health and cognition. Dr McGarry has vast experience in working with young children and researching challenges experienced in early life.

The author was inspired to write this book after gaining first-hand experience of stool withholding with her eldest child. Utilising her research skills and knowledge of developmental psychology, Dr McGarry has developed a three stage approach to tackling stool withholding that was successful with her own child. The approach incorporates research conducted on stool withholding, National Institute for Health and Care Excellence (NICE) and ERIC (The Children's Bowel & Bladder Charity) guidelines in addition to providing a deeper insight into the psychological, behavioural and sensory issues that underpin stool withholding. Dr McGarry hopes that sharing this approach will help other families and children facing this challenge.

For I

Table of Contents

Introduction

Gaining control of bowel movements is an important milestone in a child's development and one which is typically achieved in the third year of life[1]. When a child struggles with their bowel movements it can have a negative impact on their social development and result in a high degree of emotional distress[2]. If issues with bowel control are not resolved in the early years, it is possible that individuals will experience a lower health related quality of life. Furthermore, children with stool withholding and associated bowel related issues are more likely to be subjected to peer bullying and may experience long lasting psychological impacts[3]. Stool withholding does not only impact the child experiencing the condition, it can also negatively impact the family unit. Research has found that parents of children with this condition view themselves as having a lower quality of life[3] and experience an overall greater level of anxiety and worry about their child[4,5].

Despite accounting for 3-5% of general referrals within the paediatric population[6], stool withholding is often under-reported and is commonly mistreated[7,8]. This figure increases to as high as 25% when looking at gastrointestinal referrals alone[9]. The amount of referrals has had a direct impact on medical resources and has created a major challenge in clinical settings[10].

Treatment typically involves addressing the physical side of stool withholding (the constipation) and implementing positive toilet techniques[11]. However, parents are often left confused and overwhelmed as they receive little guidance on how to manage the condition and implement existing guidelines[12]. Furthermore, recent research has demonstrated the importance of addressing sensory issues when treating stool withholding[13-19]. These sensory issues are often overlooked and neglected during treatment unless a child has an existing developmental disorder such as autism spectrum disorder (ASD) or sensory processing disorder (SPD).

Children often continue to suffer with this condition throughout childhood due to the quality of the treatments implemented and the lack of support provided to parents. Stool withholding is not clearly defined and the criteria used by multiple healthcare authorities worldwide for diagnosis are not consistent[10]. One of the main barriers with diagnosing and treating stool withholding is related to how the condition is viewed. It is often referred to as childhood constipation, functional constipation, chronic constipation or faecal incontinence. The diagnosis given to a child can differ between health care practitioners. This can result in greater confusion for parents attempting to understand and manage their child's condition. The medical conditions mentioned above are very much a part of the stool withholding experience, however, they tend to be secondary symptoms which emerge as a result of the stool withholding (these will be explored further in chapter one). Therefore, purely treating these secondary conditions without addressing the root cause (i.e. the stool withholding) can result in a vicious repeating cycle of constipation and disimpaction regimes. This is a cycle that parents of children who withhold their stools often describe and one which is highly stressful and disheartening.

The purpose of this book is to help parents who have a child struggling with stool withholding to break this vicious cycle. This book will provide a supportive and practical evidence-based resource that includes the use of sensory interventions. The first chapter will provide an overview of stool withholding from common symptoms to potential causes of this condition. Research outlining the sensory contributions to stool withholding will also be explored. A three stage practical intervention that incorporates ERIC, The Children's Bowel & Bladder Charity guidelines will be outlined that aims to tackle the physical, behavioural and sensory features of stool withholding. Lastly, this book will explore how to strengthen desired responses to toileting through the use of positive reinforcement techniques. A section at the end of the book has also been included to highlight helpful medical, social media and literary resources that provide further information and support.

Chapter One

The Ins and Outs of Stool Withholding

This chapter will introduce you to stool withholding, common symptoms and the causes of this condition. A brief overview of the three stage approach to tackling stool withholding will then be outlined before being explained in detail in the subsequent chapters.

What is stool withholding?

Stool withholding is when an individual attempts to avoid a bowel motion by holding their stool in. It is also commonly referred to as functional constipation or chronic constipation. Attempting to avoid a bowel motion can temporarily relieve the urge to pass a stool but continuation of this behaviour results in the build-up of stool and stretching of the bowel. As stool accumulates in the bowel, water is absorbed which causes the stool to become hard and can lead to constipation. The hard stools become stuck or "impacted" which can lead to a condition called encopresis. Encopresis is also known as faecal incontinence or soiling and is the most common side effect of stool withholding. Liquid and softer stools leak around the impacted harder stool in the bowel resulting in soiled accidents which the child has little or no control over.

Stools build-up in the lower colon and start to harden.

The longer stools are held in the harder the stools become and the greater the build-up of stool. The colon muscles become stretched or "distended" which makes them less effective during bowel motions.

Hard stools become stuck in the colon, only liquid stools can pass at this stage. Nerves used to detect a bowel motion become desensitised and the child does not feel when they are having a soiled accident.

Illustrated by Dr. Christian Higton, Newman University, UK

What can stool withholding look like?

There are a wide range of signs and symptoms associated with stool withholding. In most cases, symptoms become more noticeable and increase in frequency and intensity the longer a stool is withheld. Some of the most common signs are discussed below.

Soiling

In most cases the child is not aware that they have soiled themselves due to the bowel nerves becoming desensitised and the colon muscles stretched. Watery stools typically leak around the hard stool or small, hard pieces of the impacted stool may be present. If the child is unable to hold a stool any longer they may have a whole bowel movement.

Crossing legs, shaking and stiffening of the body

It is usual for the child to find a hidden spot where they will cross their legs and stiffen their body in a greater effort to stop a bowel movement. A child displaying this behaviour may also have a red face from the physical effort exerted in withholding the stool.

Vacant Spells

Child may seem unresponsive and distant due to the concentration taken to withhold a stool.

Behavioural changes

The child may appear more irritable with an increase in refusal behaviours and temper tantrums. The child may also take longer to calm down and become overwhelmed in situations that they would not have previously.

Lack of energy

The child may appear lethargic and sleepy due to the energy spent on withholding a stool. This is typically seen the longer a stool is withheld.

Reduced appetite

Eating can trigger a gastrocolic reflex which initiates a bowel movement. The child may eat less in an effort to avoid this reflex. In addition, stool withholding can cause abdominal discomfort and fullness due to the accumulation of stools.

Vomiting

Persistent vomiting can occur when a complete blockage occurs in the bowel and new stool is unable to "leak" around the impacted hard stool. Medical assistance should be sought immediately if this occurs.

Swollen abdomen

The whole of the abdomen can become swollen due to the increase in stool within the bowel.

Wet accidents

As the colon becomes full and stretched it puts pressure on the bladder and can cause wet accidents. A child may have less control over their bladder due to the accumulation of hardened stool in their bowel.

Causes of stool withholding

Stool withholding behaviours have been associated with developmental disorders such as autism spectrum disorder (ASD), attention deficit hyperactivity disorder (ADHD) in addition to organic factors such as Hirschsprung's disease, muscle disorders, prior rectoanal surgery, spina bifida and hypothyroidism[2, 20, 21]. However, in most reported cases of stool withholding there are no underlying factors or organic causes that can be identified[2, 22]. Health care practitioners typically associate the onset of stool withholding with a previous experience of a hard, painful or frightening bowel movement. Following this negative experience, the child starts engaging in stool withholding behaviours in an effort to avoid bowel movements and to minimise further bad experiences when passing a stool. However, a prior negative experience of a bowel movement does not account for all cases of stool withholding and is a simplified way of viewing the condition. Stool withholding is often complex and can involve the interaction of numerous behavioural, physiological and social[23]. Recent research within this area has started to recognise the role of sensory issues in children who display stool withholding behaviours[19, 24]. In particular, a recent review suggested that heightened sensory responses (known as hyperreactivity) to touch, smell and sound and a lack of awareness of the need to pass a stool (hyporeactivity) could negatively affect a child's ability to maintain regular bowel movements and positive toileting habits[19]. Examples of sensory hyperreactivity include; distress in response to the smell of their stool, displaying pain responses when passing a stool of a normal size and consistency, fear responses towards the sound of the stool splashing in the bowl or when the toilet is flushed and describing wiping after a bowel movement as painful. The identification of these sensory issues could have a positive impact on addressing negative toileting behaviours in children, however, the contribution of sensory issues is not typically considered by clinicians when managing and treating stool withholding[19].

The three stages to tackling stool withholding

The typical treatment for stool withholding focuses on the physical side of stool withholding with the addition of positive toileting techniques. This book, however, proposes a three stage practical approach that incorporates the current treatment with the addition of techniques that are aimed at addressing potential underlying sensory issues. The first stage referred to as the physical stage tackles the physical side of stool withholding. An important stage that needs to be maintained throughout treatment. Secondly, the psychological stage addresses the different mental and emotional barriers that can contribute to a child withholding their stool. The final sensory stage addresses issues relating to heightened (hyperreactive) and reduced (hyporeactive) sensory responses within the toilet environment.

Chapter 2

The Physical Stage

If you believe your child is withholding their stool, your first step should always be to consult your GP or health care practitioner. It is important to first confirm stool withholding (or functional constipation as it is often referred to) and to rule out any other potential underlying issues. The next step is for your GP to check whether any stool is impacted (stuck in the bowel) before your child starts any treatment. This chapter will first introduce the laxatives commonly used in treating stool withholding and how they work. The disimpaction regime and how to achieve a maintenance dose, will then be outlined and is based on guidance provided by ERIC, The Children's Bowel & Bladder Charity and the National Institute for Health and Care Excellence (NICE). Website information for both of these sources can be found in the resource section at the end of this book. Lastly, dietary adjustments and their contribution to maintaining a soft stool will also be discussed in this chapter.

Laxatives

Laxatives are a type of medicine that can help an individual empty their bowels. There are two main types of laxatives that can be used for stool withholding in children, osmotic and stimulant laxatives. Osmotic laxatives are typically used for the disimpaction regime and to help maintain regular and softer bowel movements. Stimulant laxatives are normally prescribed when a child has not had a bowel movement for a significant period of time, such as a couple of weeks, or when a blockage may be suspected. Both types of laxatives will now be considered.

Osmotic laxatives

Osmotic laxatives such as lactulose (brand names include Lactugal and Dupphalac) or macrogol (brand names include Laxido, Movicol, Molaxole and CosmoCol) are typically used to treat the physical side of stool withholding on a long-term basis. Osmotic laxatives work by drawing water into the bowel which creates a softer stool. The higher the amount of laxatives taken, the softer the stool becomes and therefore easier for the child to pass.

Stimulant laxatives

Stimulant laxatives work faster than osmotic laxatives, typically within a 6- to 12-hour time period. They work by stimulating muscles in the intestines to contract and push stools along the bowel. Examples of stimulant laxatives include senna (brand name Senokot) and bisacodyl (brand name Dulcolax). Due to the stimulating nature of these laxatives, it is common for children to experience abdominal cramps whilst taking this medication.

Disimpaction Regime

If it has been confirmed that your child has an impacted stool (a stool stuck in the bowel), they will first need to go through a disimpaction regime. The disimpaction regime involves giving macrogol in large quantities in order to remove all of the hardened stool accumulated in the bowel.

Despite the recommended dosing being spread out over a week, it is important to note that disimpaction could be achieved sooner or later than this time period. The time taken depends on the amount of accumulated stool and the length of time it has been in the bowel for. The aim of disimpaction is to achieve a watery stool consistency, i.e. light brown water with some brown bits in it, on at least two occasions. If you are unsure whether the stool is watery enough, it is better to carry on with the higher dose for another day to ensure the backlog of stool has been cleared. Long term use of macrogols and higher doses of osmotic laxatives are not harmful to your child and will not cause the bowel to become lazy. If disimpaction has not been achieved after two weeks, the NICE guidelines recommend the addition of a stimulant laxative to speed up the disimpaction process. Some GPs recommend the introduction of the stimulant laxative earlier, depending on your child's situation, so it is important to follow guidance provided by your health care practitioner.

Table 1 outlines the macrogol daily dosages as recommended by the NICE Guidelines on constipation in children and young people.

Table 1
NICE Guidelines
Recommended daily macrogol sachets for
disimpaction

Day	Under 1 year	1-5 years	5-12 years
1	½-1	2	4
2	½-1	4	6
3	½-1	4	8
4	½-1	6	10
5	. ½-1	6	12
6	½-1	8	12
7	½-1	8	12

What to expect

When your child is undergoing a disimpaction regime it can be hard to know what to expect. The experience will differ between children and can depend on the length of time your child has been withholding their stool. The most commonly reported experiences are explored further below.

An increase in soiling and wet accidents

Due to the increase of softer stool, there will be a greater amount of "overflow stool" that will initially leak around the impacted stool in the bowel. As there is an increase in volume of stool in the bowel, this can put more pressure on the bladder which can increase the amount of wet accidents a child may have.

Soft and hard stools

As the disimpaction regime progresses, it is normal to see lumps of hard stool mixed in with liquid stools. This is a sign that the disimpaction is working. The lumps are pieces of the impacted stool that are being broken down.

Increase in stools

As higher doses of macrogol are given, more stools will be produced. If your child is toilet trained, they will experience frequent trips to the toilet and potentially an increase in soiling as previously explained. If your child is wearing nappies you will need to keep a close eye on them and ensure that they are being changed regularly to avoid nappy leakages.

Abdominal discomfort

Your child may experience discomfort as they attempt to hold in the increased volume of watery stool. In addition, discomfort can arise from the impacted stool being broken down and moved along the bowel.

Maintenance Dose

Once disimpaction has been achieved (brown watery stool without lumps on at least two occasions), a maintenance dose will need to be established. Even though the hardened stool has been cleared, the maintenance dose of macrogols is needed to ensure that stool does not reaccumulate and to allow the bowel to regain its shape after being stretched. The guidance for a maintenance dose (recommended by NICE[25]) is shown in table 2.

Table 2
NICE guidelines
Macrogol sachets per day for maintenance dose

Child Age	Sachets per Day
Under a year	½ -1
1-5 years	1-4
5-12 years	2-4

The consistency of the stool will take a few days to settle so NICE recommend that the first maintenance dose is provided for a week before adjusting. The aim of the maintenance dose is to achieve a smooth, soft, sausage shape stool at least once a day. This type of stool is also known as a "Type 4" stool on the Bristol Stool Chart[26]. The Bristol Stool Chart is commonly used by clinicians to diagnose constipation and diarrhoea. Type 1 and 2 stools are typically classed as constipation and type 6 and 7 stools are usually diagnosed as diarrhoea.

Bristol Stool Chart

Type 1
Individual hard lumps, like nuts

Type 2
Sausage-shaped but lumpy

Type 3
Like a sausage but with cracks on the surface

Type 4
Like a sausage, smooth and soft

Type 5
Soft blobs with clear cut edges

Type 6
A mushy stool with fluffy pieces and ragged edges

Type 7
Entirely liquid with no solid pieces

Illustrated by Dr. Christian Higton, Newman University

You will need to monitor your child's stools closely using the Bristol Stool Chart as a guide. The maintenance dose will need to be increased if your child is producing a stool that is too hard/too infrequent. If your child is producing stools that are too loose and watery then the maintenance dose will need to be reduced. It is likely that your child will need to stay on macrogols for a prolonged period of time (months or even years) and slowly weaned off to ensure that they are still able to produce a daily, soft stool.

Moving Forward

For a child who withholds their stools it is unlikely that they will automatically revert to producing a daily stool after a disimpaction regime. This is where behavioural and sensory interventions are needed to break the stool withholding cycle. Furthermore, due to the stretching of the bowel, your child may not know when they need to pass a stool for a few weeks to even a couple of months following disimpaction. This makes it extremely hard to monitor stool consistency and to understand whether they are on the correct maintenance dose. It is therefore advised that the maintenance dose provided is half of the dose that was needed to achieve disimpaction in your child. For example, if it took 8 sachets to achieve disimpaction for your child you would then give 4 sachets daily. If you find that your child is consistently soiling themselves on this dose then it can be reduced. This maintenance dosage should be used alongside the behavioural and sensory techniques outlined in the following chapters. Once your child is successfully engaging with the counting technique (described in chapter 4) the maintenance dose should be reviewed to ensure they are easily able to produce stools.

Macrogol tips

As this type of laxative works by binding with water, it is important to prepare the correct amount of water before adding it to anything otherwise the macrogol will not work. The usual dose is approximately 62.5mls per sachet, but always check the instructions as amounts can differ depending on brand. A second important consideration is ensuring that your child stays hydrated whilst taking macrogol. The macrogol water is not absorbed by the body as it is drawn directly into the bowel. Any macrogol water can therefore not be included in your child's daily fluid intake. Furthermore, it can be difficult ensuring that your child takes the dose they should be, especially during a disimpaction regime. Below are some suggestions of how to encourage your child to take their macrogol:

- Mix the macrogol water with squash or fresh fruit juices.
- To "dampen" the taste of the macrogol you can mix it and store it in the fridge for an hour before use. Laxido will last up to 6 hours after mixing and Movicol will last for 24 hours.
- Macrogol water can be added to anything and used in a variety of ways. For example, you can make macrogol jelly, ice lollies and

even porridge. Have a think about what your child likes to eat and think about how you could add the macrogol water to it.

- Make the macrogol drinks fun by using new cups and fun straws. Take part in different drinking games with your child, for example, who can finish their drink first or everyone takes a drink when a certain word is said in a song.

Dietary Considerations

Dietary fibre plays an important role in helping our bodies to create soft stools that are easy to pass. NICE guidelines[25] recommend that dietary interventions should be used alongside a laxative treatment but never alone as a first-line treatment. In order to increase your child's daily intake of fibre, it is important for them to be eating a range of fruits and vegetables. Some examples of high fibre fruit and vegetables include carrots, broccoli, avocado, raspberries, bananas and strawberries. In addition, substituting refined grains such as white bread, pasta and rice for wholegrain alternatives is also a great way of increasing daily fibre. However, it can be difficult to make dietary changes in children who withhold their stools as they may have reduced appetites and be particular about what they eat. Here are some suggestions of how to increase fruit and vegetable intake:

- Take your child to the fruit and vegetable aisles and let them pick what they would like to try.
- Make funny faces and pictures out of different fruit for snack time. Cookie and biscuit stencils are a quick way to create lots of different and fun pictures.
- Be creative with your cooking. For example, blend vegetables to make a pasta sauce full of hidden vegetables.
- Involve your child in fruit picking and growing vegetables. There are many "grow your own" vegetable packs aimed at young children.

Chapter 3

The Psychological Stage

Your child may be experiencing different emotional and mental barriers that are contributing to their stool withholding behaviours. The whole process of having a bowel movement, from feeling the urge to pass a stool to producing one can be a confusing and anxiety provoking experience for a child. Different barriers can include:

- Fears and anxieties relating to passing a stool.
- Uncertainties about the process.
- Lacking confidence in toileting abilities.
- Potential power struggles where your child is eager to exercise their independence.
- Feeling uncomfortable in the toilet environment.

The aim of the psychological stage is to address different potential barriers by normalising the entire process. This can be achieved through the use of stories, having conversations with your child, by modelling positive behaviour and from establishing a positive toilet routine.

Stories

Stories are a fantastic way to teach your child about the ins and outs of the digestive system. There are a wide range of toddler and child orientated books that look at the *how's* and *why's* of pooing. If your child likes reading stories with you, this can be a really fun and engaging way for them to understand more about how their bodies work, their anatomy and why it is important to eat well. There are a number of books which are tailored specifically towards children who withhold their stools, please see the resource section towards the end of the book for some recommended examples. By reading these stories with your child, not only are you educating them about the process and importance of passing a stool in a way that they can relate to, you are also demystifying the process for them.

Talking to your child

In some cases, the easiest way to understand how your child is feeling is simply to ask them. Even with young children you can ask how they feel about pooing and if anything worries them about it. However, even at a young age, children are very good at knowing what adults want to hear and providing answers that they think will please them. If a child has been withholding a stool for a prolonged period of time, it is likely that they will know that this is a behaviour that you do not approve of, so they may not express any negative feelings about pooing for fear of disappointing you. At this stage you just need to reassure your child that they can talk to you about anything and that you are always happy to hear how they are feeling. Encouraging your child to talk about feelings and anxieties surrounding stool withholding can emerge in different ways, for example, through positive role modelling and play. These scenarios are explored in more detail in the next sections.

Modelling positive toileting behaviour

Children learn a lot from observing how their parents behave and how they approach different situations. Talking freely in your house about your toilet experiences and encouraging these conversations with your child is a great way to normalise pooing. Talking about your own experiences in a funny and positive way can encourage your child to open up about their toilet experiences, especially if they are normally reluctant to talk about them. For example, "My stomach felt a bit grumbly and was making all these noises *grumble rumble grumble* so I went and sat on the toilet to see if I needed a poo. Do you know what? I did! I made all these funny noises and my tummy feels so good now! Does your tummy ever make those noises?".

Play

Creative and imaginative play is a crucial part of child development. Children are able to use play to develop vital skills that help them to problem solve and to share their thoughts and feelings[27]. Play can be very helpful in the context of stool withholding as it can help your child express how they are feeling and identify concerns they have. Below are two examples of games you can play with your child.

Poo Dough

This creative game teaches your child about how food is turned into poo in a fun and interactive way. For this game you'll need play dough (ideally a few different colours), a plastic sandwich bag and scissors (for use by the adult only). Ask your child what food they want to make out of play dough. Once you have made your play dough food, explain to your child that you are going to see what happens when you eat food. Get your child to pretend to eat the play dough food with it falling into their pretend sandwich bag tummy. Explain to your child how food is broken down in their tummy and how it moves into their intestines where it gets squashed together. Act out how this happens with your child also helping. Once the play dough food has been fully squashed and mixed up, cut a small hole in the corner of the sandwich bag tummy. Explain to your child that this is where the poo comes out and show them how to squeeze the bag to produce different poos. You can play this game with different play dough food, showing how stools can look different each time in terms of colour, consistency and size. This game is great for helping children understand their own anatomy and the process behind passing a stool.

Baby won't poo!

This game relies on imaginative play and allows your child to exercise their problem solving abilities. In addition, children will often use objects and play scenarios to express feelings that they are struggling to communicate. This game could help provide a useful insight into the particular issues and anxieties your child may be facing in regards to stool withholding. In this game you will need to guide your child through a role play with a baby doll. Show your child the doll and explain that they have tummy ache and ask what you should do. If your child is struggling to understand the issue presented provide prompts such as "I think baby might need a poo!". Guide your child through the game asking how you can help baby poo. Ask your child how baby might be feeling and make sure you ask your child to explain why baby might be feeling a particular way. In addition, encourage your child to provide solutions to help baby poo and make baby feel better.

Toilet routines

Within this stage, it is important to establish a positive and empowering toilet routine for your child. This means creating a toilet routine which they have an element of control in to help address issues related to your child asserting their independence. Look at suggestions in chapter 5 (reinforcement of behaviours) for tips on how to empower your child. In addition, creating a positive toilet routine will also help to normalise the process of passing a stool. Your child will start to learn that sitting on the toilet is just a normal part of their day.

Creating a positive toilet routine

Choose a time for your child to sit on the toilet that works with their normal routine. This ideally should be the same time each day, for example, 5-10 minutes after dinner. This can be increased to twice a day (perhaps after breakfast) once a sitting routine has been established and accepted. If your child is struggling to sit on the toilet for the length of time suggested simply reduce the time to one more suitable for them. You can start to increase the time once they become more comfortable sitting on the toilet. The emphasis should be on getting your child to sit on the toilet and NOT on passing a stool, as this can create unintentional pressure and can overwhelm your child. Create a fun positive toileting environment through reading stories, watching their tablet, playing music and using bubbles. Playing games with your child while they sit on the toilet is also a great way to reduce anxiety. Some fun examples include Simon says and sitting dancing games. Once your child has sat on the toilet make sure you praise them and provide positive reinforcement. Examples of useful positive reinforcement techniques are covered in chapter 5 (reinforcement of behaviours).

Chapter 4

The Sensory stage

In addition to physical and psychological factors, heightened (hyperreactive) and reduced (hyporeactive) sensory responses within the toilet environment can contribute towards stool withholding behaviours[13- 19.] The first stage in addressing these sensory issues is to identify the hyperreactive and/or hyporeactive behaviours your child is displaying. This can be achieved through observing your child in their toileting environment and through conversations with them. Sensory issues may change over time or become more pronounced the longer your child holds onto a stool. There are eight different senses: tactile, visual, auditory, olfactory, gustatory, vestibular, proprioception and interoception. Common issues within these senses will be identified alongside practical suggestions for helping your child tackle each one.

Tactile

Physical sensations from the toileting environment can create feelings of discomfort or uncertainty for a child. Surfaces within the bathroom can feel cold or hard to the touch. In addition, some children may be sensitive to the sensation of toilet roll when wiping.

Discomfort when sitting on a toilet

Introduce a child's toilet seat that can be inserted onto the adult seat. Different shapes are also available that may be more comfortable for your child. In addition, some inserts are padded which could provide a softer alternative.

Use of toilet paper or wipes

Different brands of toilet roll and wipes have a variety of textures. Some children may find toilet roll too rough or wipes too cold or wet. Experiment with softer alternatives or even store wipes in a warmer place before use.

Cold surfaces

Walking on a cold floor and sitting on a cold seat can create an uninviting toilet environment for your child. Ensuring a warmer temperature in your bathroom can help to combat these issues. Consider the use of bathmats and toilet mats to create a warmer and softer walk way to the toilet.

Visual

Visual stimulation within the toileting environment can be extremely overwhelming for your child, especially if they are displaying hyperreactive behaviours. Bright lighting, busy decorations, reflections and general bathroom clutter can result in a visual overload.

Lighting

Battery powered lamps offer a softer and more appealing lighting solution. There are a number of child friendly options that come in a variety of fun shapes. Many are touch sensitive lights that change colour, offering a fun and interactive element for your child. Special toilet bowl lights are also available and normally in a variety of colours. This can help remove the mystery element of the toilet by illuminating it and again they add softer lighting to the environment.

Decoration

Opt to use a bathroom in your house that has less decoration. If this is not an option, you can cover busy floors and tiles with plain towels or throws. There may be a specific colour that your child likes and finds calming.

Reflections

Covering mirrors with towels or throws. This can reduce light and physical reflections which can add to visual stimulation.

Clutter

Visual overload can occur if your child has too much visual stimulation, for example, if there are a lot of objects to look at in your bathroom. De-clutter your bathroom by clearing away toiletries/cleaning products or by using closed opaque storage boxes.

Auditory

There are a variety of sounds that a child can be exposed to within the bathroom environment, from running water and extractor fans to toilet flushes. Sounds can often be sudden, loud and echo which can be particularly distressful.

Echoes

Introducing more soft furnishings such as towels and toilet/sink mats to reduce echoes.

Splash from stool

Toilet paper can be folded and put into the toilet basin. This will stop the stool from splashing and reduce the noise produced.

Toilet flush

If your child has shown a negative reaction to the toilet flush, avoid flushing while your child is on the toilet or even close to it. When your child becomes more comfortable in the bathroom you can start to gradually introduce flushing the toilet when your child is by the exit to the room. This should reduce the intrusiveness of the sound and the volume.

Extractor fan

Extractor fans can produce a relaxing white noise effect for your child or alternatively they can be viewed as an intrusive and strange noise. As extractor fans tend to start when lights are turned on in bathrooms the start of the noise can create a shock and be very noticeable. Turning off the extractor fan is a good way to create a seamless transition between rooms and to reduce the novelty of the bathroom.

Olfactory and gustatory

Toiletries and cleaning products commonly used in bathrooms typically have strong scents which can impact olfactory (smells) and gustatory (taste) senses. Going to the bathroom can become an overwhelming or distressing experience for a child when they are faced with a variety of strong smells. Some children may also find the smell of their stools unpleasant.

Perfumed toiletries and air fresheners

Eliminate the use of perfumed products or minimise the use of different smelling products in the bathroom space. You could also allow your child to be involved in picking a scent that they like and recognise.

Cleaning products

Using odour neutralising products. Avoiding deep cleaning bathrooms during a time your child would be around and willing to use to the bathroom. Keeping the bathroom well ventilated and using extractor fans if available (when the child is not using the bathroom).

Smell of stool

Use special stool neutralising sprays which can be put in the toilet basin before your child uses it. This will dramatically reduce the smell of any stools produced. Encourage your child to pick out a smell that they like or find comforting. For example, this could be a candle, particular toy or a snack they like. Allow your child to hold this item and sniff it while sitting on the toilet.

Vestibular

The vestibular sense is essentially related to our balance and how we move in different spaces[28]. This sense allows us to maintain our balance whilst engaging in different tasks such as sitting on a toilet. A child with vestibular sensitivities may dislike activities which involve them being picked up or where they are unable to control their own body within a space, for example, on swings. This can extend to a child feeling unsteady on a toilet and having anxieties relating to maintaining their balance.

Feeling unsteady on the toilet

Child toilet seats are a great way to help your child feel more steady on a toilet. Ones are available with smaller holes which provide greater support. The use of a foot stool will help your child achieve a more comfortable and steady position on the toilet. A variety of child friendly weighted lap pads are also available. The pressure exerted from these pads can help a child feel grounded and more secure when sitting on the toilet through increasing sensations in the legs. Handrails positioned next to the toilet can also provide children with a physical sense of security. There is a wide selection of temporary pop-up handrails or wall suction ones that would be suitable for a bathroom environment.

Refusal to sit on the toilet

4-in-1 potties are a useful alternative for children who refuse to sit on a toilet. They are lower to the ground and usually include features such as handles to help your child feel more secure. Some children may feel more comfortable in a squat position, alternatives such as squatty potty can be helpful in these scenarios.

Proprioception

Proprioception is the sense that is also known as body awareness[29]. This sense provides us with the information we need to interact with objects in our environment, for example, how much force to exert in relation to different objects. Proprioception is also related to our coordination skills and allows us to understand the positioning of our different body parts without looking at them. Children with increased proprioception sensitivities within the toileting environment may experience heightened sensations in regards to passing a stool or from sitting on a toilet. Experiences may be reported as painful or uncomfortable. Additionally, children with a reduced proprioception sensitivity may be less aware of different bodily sensations. As a result, they may prefer to wear their nappy while passing a stool to stimulate a feeling of deep pressure.

Heightened proprioception sensitivity

See suggestions under tactile sense at the beginning of the chapter as these will also help here. The use of an osmotic laxative to increase the softness of the stool will be helpful as your child will be used to the sensation of a harder, more formed stool. Changing to a very soft and less formed stool will change the sensation and discomfort experienced when they have a bowel movement. This will also make it easier for your child to produce a stool when done in line with the "counting method", covered in the interoception section below.

Reduced proprioception sensitivity

If your child avoids passing a stool unless they are wearing a nappy you can encourage them to sit on the toilet with their nappy on. Once your child is used to sitting on the toilet you can start to cut small holes in the base of their nappy to allow it to pass into the toilet. Gradual increases in hole size can help your child to adjust to the concept of producing a stool in the toilet. You can also start to gradually reduce the "tightness" of the nappy they wear and even cut away parts of the nappy over time. Providing your child with more tight fitting clothes (even over a nappy) will provide them with a greater sensation of pressure. You can also offer weighted lap pads to your child as this will exert pressure and extra sensation on their legs. This will also help them to feel more secure on the toilet. Children with reduced proprioception sensitivity may commonly place themselves against the cistern or the wall that the toilet is on. This is done again to increase sensation on their body and to create a better understanding of where their body is in relation to the toilet. Rolling up a towel or placing a yoga mat behind them is a useful way to provide further sensation but will also to help them place themselves in a better position that is more secure.

Interoception

Interoception is our ability to perceive different physical sensations relating to internal processes within our bodies[30]. Different examples include understanding when we are tired, hungry and also when we need to go to the toilet. For some children who have engaged in stool withholding behaviours, their bowel can become stretched (distended) and they can lose tone in their rectum. This can reduce the efficiency of the muscles in the colon and desensitise nerve endings. As a result, the typical signals that tell you that you need to pass a stool do not work as well as they should do[23]. For children with a distended bowel it is likely that they experience a reduced awareness of the urge pass a stool.

The counting method

The purpose of the counting method is to teach the "mechanical" side of passing a stool. This should help your child learn how to initiate bowel movements and how to control them. This method works by incorporating squeezes into your child's toilet routine to create a new learnt behaviour whereby every time they visit the toilet they complete squeezes.

1) Once a positive toilet routine has been established the counting method can be implemented before the child finishes their session on the toilet.

2) Encourage your child to do 10 bottom squeezes (or pushes depending on what your child responds to) that are counted with the adult. You can explain squeezes in terms of how they can make their bottom move, for example, when you do a big cough or when you push down from your tummy.

3) Squeezes should be presented as a game and linked to the child's counting ability if possible. It is important to be creative with how you present the bottom squeezes to your child through the use of games such as

Simon says and fun challenges, for example, "I bet you can't do a squeeze as big as me!".

4) The number of squeezes should be increased once the child is used to the routine of doing this method.

5) Your child should be praised and rewarded after completing their toilet time and squeezes.

The aim and focus is to complete the squeezes and NOT to poo. Once your child is confident in doing their squeezes the focus can then move onto encouraging the passing of a stool using the steps outlined below.

6) Close observation of stool softener/laxative/dietary changes to ensure the stool is around a type 4 on the Bristol Stool Form Scale. This will mean that the stool should naturally start to come out with squeezes and as your child builds up their muscle tone.

7) If stools are not coming out with squeezes a gradual increase in osmotic laxatives (to a type 5 or type 6 stool) is beneficial to ensure minimal effort is required from the child to produce a stool.

From engaging in the counting method and following the steps above, your child should start to learn the association between squeezes and passing a stool. Due to the softness of the stool and the focus being on squeezes, your child should start to form a positive association between squeezes and passing a stool.

Chapter 5

Reinforcements of behaviours

Once physical, psychological and sensory issues have been identified the aim is to address each one via the methods discussed in previous chapters. One issue remains at this stage though, how do you encourage a child to engage with these solutions? The answer is positive reinforcement techniques. Reinforcement techniques build a positive and consistent approach for your child that will empower them and teach them how to handle their emotions in a healthy way.

Empowering your child

The key to empowering your child is to listen to them and to help them feel heard. Problem solve with your child by asking them for suggestions and listening to their ideas. Through problem solving with your child and involving them in the process you are in turn empowering them. This can help your child to feel a certain sense of control and will encourage them to take part in the process. For example, if your child has a sensitivity to the general toileting environment, let them show you where they want to put their potty, the type of potty they want to use and the items they want around them.

Emotion regulation

Stool withholding can be extremely stressful for children and can give rise to a range of emotions that may be confusing or hard for them to process. Through teaching and modelling emotion regulation techniques you can help your child to understand their emotions, how to respond to them and in turn create a safe space for them. The RULER method (developed by the Yale Center for Emotional Intelligence in 2005) is a commonly used approach in social and emotional learning which is used to help children Recognise, Understand, Label, Express and Regulate their emotions. Numerous studies have shown that children who have taken part in RULER programs are more effective at managing their emotions, are better problem solvers and are less depressed and anxious[31]. The RULER method can be applied in a variety of scenarios, but imagine the following example where you find your child hiding and crossing their legs as they actively try to withhold their stool. When you suggest going to the toilet or try to talk to them your child becomes very upset or angry. In this scenario you could take the following approach using the RULER method:

1) Recognising emotion

Go down to your child's level and tell them that you can see that they are upset.

2) Understanding the cause of the emotion

Show your child that you understand why they may be feeling upset. This will vary on the individual child and situation but examples include, the child feeling scared of passing a stool, or feeling scared of going into the bathroom, or not understanding the sensations they are experiencing. Through identifying the factors contributing to the emotion, your child will also start to understand more clearly why they are feeling upset too.

3) Labelling the emotion

Label the emotion or emotions your child is displaying to help them understand what they are experiencing. For example, are they scared, angry or sad? Once a label has been attached to a feeling you can begin to figure out what to do about it together.

4) Expressing the emotion

Help your child to express how they are feeling and reassure them that it is good to show how they feel. For younger children or high emotion situations it is sometimes useful to show a visual scale of faces with different emotions such as sad, happy, angry and calm for your child to point to.

5) Regulating the emotion

Use positive language, touch and tone to reassure your child. Once the emotion they are experiencing has been labelled you can work together to problem solve how they can feel better and thus regulate their emotion. Within this scenario, suggestions of different things which could be done in the toilet environment is a possibility. If your child appears upset by suggestions, attempt to redirect their attention by focusing on things in the environment around them or by talking about a TV show they like or an activity they are fond of.

Positive reinforcement techniques

Positive reinforcement works by providing a reward or desirable outcome after your child engages in a behaviour that you want to encourage. By providing a reward for a behaviour, it is more likely that your child will repeat this behaviour in the future. Talk to your child, find out what motivates them and what they would like as a reward. Sticker charts are a fantastic way of providing an immediate reward for a behaviour whilst also allowing your child to track their progress and build towards achieving a toy or trip that they want. It is important to identify small and achievable goals that can be built upon. For example, sitting on the toilet (perhaps with a tablet) for a minute to progressing to sitting on the toilet and doing squeezes. If your child does not manage to achieve a goal at any point avoid negative feedback or pressuring your child. Children are extremely perceptive and can pick up on frustrations that you may be experiencing, this can in turn contribute to confidence issues and unintentionally reinforce withholding behaviours. Instead, re-evaluate goals set, talk to your child and think about how you could approach the scenario differently.

Chapter 6

The Bottom line

Stool withholding can often be a complex condition that can impact children in many ways. The approaches outlined in this book look at the physical, psychological and sensory contributions to stool withholding and explore practical ways in which to tackle them. From reading this book, you have already taken the first steps towards overcoming this condition and providing your child with the tools they need to conquer their stool withholding. Approaches can take time and patience to implement. Once you start including them in your child's daily routine you can start to identify what your child responds to and where certain approaches could be tweaked to suit your child's needs further. Each child is different and will progress at their own pace. Some children will respond to some approaches better than others, and that's okay. You know your child the best, keep communicating with them, listen to them and problem solve together.

During this process remember to take the time to be patient with yourself. Although the focus of this book is on your child and the impact stool withholding can have on them, the condition can also be very hard for the caregivers and family unit. Some moments you may find harder than others, seek support and talk to others. Stool withholding is very common in young children, you may be surprised at how many other parents are also struggling with this condition.

Overcoming stool withholding is not an easy journey, but it is an achievable one. Each child is different and will experience this journey in their own way, where some days will be better than others. Keep the line of communication open with your child, constantly assess their progress, be open to adjusting the approach taken and remain consistent in your support and reassurance.

Resources

There are a variety of resources available that are aimed at providing parents with information about stool withholding. The medical resources have frequently been referred to throughout this book and I have identified additional resources that should help build on the topics covered.

Medical

The medical resources mentioned in this section are a good starting point for learning about stool withholding and support options offered by health care practitioners. These websites are particularly useful at explaining what stool withholding is and the common behaviours associated with the condition. In addition, physical treatments for stool withholding (such as laxative dosage and disimpaction regimes) are also explored in detail. The NHS website provides information on childhood constipation and outlines support avenues within their service. Information provided by ERIC, The Children's Bowel & Bladder Charity outlines positive reinforcement techniques and common problems faced in toilet training. ERIC and Bladder & Bowel UK have also produced a range of booklets (free and available to download) which provide in-depth information and support on stool withholding in children. If you are looking for medical guidelines on treating and diagnosing stool withholding, these can be found on the National Institute for Health and Care Excellence (NICE) website.

Provider	Website
NHS	https://www.nhs.uk/conditions/baby/health/constipation-in-children/
ERIC, The Children's Bowel & Bladder Charity	https://eric.org.uk/childrens-bowels/stool-withholding/
Bladder & Bowel UK	https://www.bbuk.org.uk/children-young-people/resources-for-children/

Social Media

Social media can be a fantastic way of accessing information and support from a community that are experiencing similar issues as you. In particular, there are Instagram and Facebook accounts set up by health care professionals that focus specifically on issues with toilet training and promoting healthy eating habits in younger children. From top tips on toilet training to creating simple but healthy food for your little one is easy to find if you know where to look. Following and interacting with these accounts can give you direct access to the experts and can be a great way of building a unique and responsive support network.

Books

In chapter 3 (The Psychological Stage) I outlined how stories can help you explore stool withholding with your child. Some of the books below are written specifically for children who suffer from this condition. These books are an excellent resource to use with your child to help them navigate this condition.

Book Title	Author
I can't, I won't, No Way!	Tracey J. Vessillo
It Hurts When I Poop!: A Story for Children Who are Scared to Use the Potty	Howard J. Bennet and M. S. Weber
Dash's Belly Ache: A book for children who can't or won't poop	Wendy Hayden
How Do You Poo?	Allison Jandu
Every Body Poops: Poopy's Great Adventure Through the Body and Beyond	Colleen A. Simons and Diogo Alves

References

1) Schum, T. R., Kolb, T. M., McAuliff, T. L., Simms, M. D., Underhill, R. L., & Lewis, M. (2002). Sequential acquisition of toilet-training skills: A descriptive study of gender and age differences in normal children. *Pediatrics, 109,* 1–7.

2) Beaudry-Bellefeuille, I., & Lane, S. J. (2017). Examining sensory overresponsiveness in preschool children with retentive fecal incontinence. *American Journal of Occupational Therapy, 71* (5), 1-8.

3) Kovacic, K., Sood., M. R., Mugie, S., Lorenzo, C. D., Nurko, S. Heinz., N., et al. (2015). A multicentre study on childhood constipation and fecal incontinence: effects on quality of life. *The Journal of Pediatrics, 166* (6), 1482-1487.

4) Wang, C., Shang, L., Zhang, Y., Tian, J., Wang, B., Yang, X., et al., (2013). Impact of functional constipation on health-related quality of life in preschool children and their

families in Xi'an, China. *PLoS One, 8* (10), e77273.

5) Kaugars, A. S., Silverman, A., Kinservik, M., Heinze, S., Reinemann, L., Sander, M., et al., (2010). Families' perspectives on the effect of constipation and fecal incontinence on quality of life. *Journal of Pediatric Gastroenterology and Nutrition, 51,* 747–752.

6) Mutyala, R., Sanders, K., & Bates, M.D. (2020) Assessment and management of pediatric constipation for the primary care clinician. *Current Problems in Pediatric and Adolescent Health Care, 50,* 100802.

7) Cohn, A. (2010). Stool withholding. *Journal of Pediatric Neurology, 8,* 29-30.

8) National Institute for Health and Car Excellence (2020). *Constipation in children: Doses and titration of laxatives.* Clarity Informatics Limited. https://cks.nice.org.uk/topics/constipation-in-children/prescribing-information/doses-titration/

9) National Collaborating Centre for Women's and Children's Health (2010) *Constipation in children and young people: diagnosis and management of idiopathic childhood constipation in primary and secondary care (full NICE guideline).* Royal College of Obstetricians and Gynaecologists. http://www.nice.org.uk

10) Rajindrajith, S., Devanarayana, N. M., Perera, B. J. C., & Benninga, M. A. (2016). Childhood constipation as an emerging public health problem. *World Journal of Gastroenterology, 22* (30), 6864-6875.

11) Ali, S. R., Ahmed, S. Qadir, M., Humayun, K. N., & Ahmad., K. (2011). Fecal Incontinence and Constipation in Children: A Clinical Conundrum. *Oman Medical Journal, 26* (5), 376-378.

12) Von Gontard, A. & Neveus, T. (2006). Management of Disorders of Bladder and Bowel Control in Childhood. UK, Wiley.

13) Bakker, M. J., Boer, F., Benninga, M. A., Koelman2, H. T. M., Tijssen, M. A. J. (2010). Increased auditory startle reflex in children

with functional abdominal pain. *The Journal of paediatrics, 156* (2), 285-291.

14) Beaudry-Bellefeuille, I., Schaaf, R. C., & Polo, E. R. (2013). Occupational Therapy Based on Ayres Sensory Integration in the Treatment of Retentive Fecal Incontinence in a 3-Year-Old Boy. *American Journal of Occupational Therapy, 67* (5), 601-606.

15) Beaudry-Bellefeuille, I. (2014). Examining the Sensory Characteristics of Preschool Children with Retentive Fecal Incontinence. MSc Thesis, Virginia Commonwealth University.

16) Beaudry-Bellefeuille, I., & Ramos-Polo, E. (2011). Tratamiento combinado de la retención voluntaria de heces mediante fármacos y terapia ocupacional [Combined treatment of voluntary stool retention with medication and occupational therapy]. *Boletin de pediatria, 51* (217), 169-176.

17) Mazurek, M. O., Vasa, R. A., Kalb, L. G., et al. (2013) Anxiety, sensory over-responsivity, and gastrointestinal problems in children with

autism spectrum disorders. *Journal of Abnormal Psychology, 41* (1), 165–176.

18) Pollock, M. R., Metz, A. E., & Barabash, T. (2014). Association between dysfunction elimination syndrome and sensory processing disorder. *The American journal of occupational therapy, 68* (4), 472-477.

19) Beaudry-Bellefeuille, I., Lane, S. J., & Lane, A. E. (2019). Sensory integration concerns in children with functional defecation disorders: A scoping review. *American Journal of Occupational Therapy, 73* (3), 7303205050p1–7303205050p13.

20) McElhanon, B. O., McCracken, C., Karpen, S., & Sharp, W. G. (2014). Gastrointestinal symptoms in autism spectrum disorder: A meta-analysis. *Pediatrics, 133*, 872–883.

21) McKeown, C., Hisle-Gorman, E., Eide, M., Gorman, G. H., & Nylund, C. M. (2013). Association of constipation and fecal incontinence with attention-deficit/ hyperactivity disorder. *Pediatrics, 132*, e1210–e1215.

22) Tabbers, M. M., DiLorenzo, C., Berger, M. Y., Faure, C., Langendam, M. W., & Nurko, S., (2014). Evaluation and treatment of functional constipation in infants and children: Evidence-based recommendations from ESPGHAN and NASPGHAN. *Journal of Pediatric Gastroenterology and Nutrition, 58,* 258–274.

23) Freeman, K. A., Riley, A., Duke, D. C., & Fu, R. (2014). Systematic review and meta-analysis of behavioral interventions for fecal incontinence with constipation. *Journal of Pediatric Psychology, 39,* 887–902.

24) Handley-More, D., Richards, K., Macauley, R., & Tierra, A. (2009). Encopresis: Multi-disciplinary management. *Journal of Occupational Therapy, Schools and Early Intervention, 2,* 96–102.

25) National Institute for Health and Care Excellence (updated 2022). *CG99 Constipation in children and young people diagnosis and management of idiopathic childhood constipation in primary and*

secondary care. National Collaborating Centre of Women's and Children's Health.

26) Lewis, S. J., & Heaton, K. W. (1997). Stool form scale as a useful guide to intestinal transit time. *Scandinavian Journal of Gastroenterology, 32,* 920-924.

27) Jaggy, A., Kalkusch, I., Burkhardt Bossi, C., Weiss, B., Sticca, F., & Perren., S. (2023). The impact of social pretend play on preschoolers' social development: Results of an experimental study. *Early Childhood Research Quarterly, 64* (3). 13-25.

28) Wiener-Vacher, S. R., Hamilton, D. A., & Wiener, S. I. (2013). Vestibular activity and cognitive development in children: perspectives. *Frontiers in integrative neuroscience, 92* (7).

29) Holst-Wolf, J. M., Yeh, I., & Konczak, J. (2016). Development of Proprioceptive Acuity in Typically Developing Children: Normative Data on Forearm Position Sense. *Frontiers in human neuroscience, 10* (436).

30) Barrett L. F., Quigley K., Bliss-Moreau E., & Aronson K. (2004). Interoceptive sensitivity and self-reports of emotional experience. *Journal of Personality and Social Psychology,* 87, 684–697.

31) Brackett, M. A., Rivers, S, E., Reyes, M. R., & Salovey, P. (2012). Enhacning academic performance and social and emotional competence with the RULER feeling word curriculum. *Learning and Individual Differences, 22* (2), 218-224.

Printed in Great Britain
by Amazon

25047657R00046